Little Miss Spider

David C. Putnam

ISBN 10:	Hardcover	1-4257-3800-1
	Softcover	1-4257-3799-4
ISBN 13:	Hardcover	978-1-4257-3800-6
	Softcover	978-1-4257-3799-3

This book was printed in the United States of America.

To order additional copies of this book, contact:
Xlibris Corporation
1-888-795-4274
www.Xlibris.com
Orders@Xlibris.com
36583

Little Miss Spider

CONTENTS

Forward.. 9

Striving for Personal Worth.. 11
To Catch a Falling Star 12
Born in the Free World.. 13
Principles of Pride 14
Chimes of Freedom 15
Will Someday Ever Come 16
One More Light 17
Turn the Light On 18
Embracing for Life.. 19
A World of Color... 20
Intruder 21
Inside the Wall 22
Chairs.. 23
Looking for a Peace of Mind... 24
Emptiness of Birth 25
Terminally Ill 26
Crying From Heaven 27
Sierra Leone Amputee 28
A Quake in the City 29
A Civilization Savaged.. 30
Echo's of Starvation 32
In the Glooming of the Moon Light.. 33
Walking Into Age 34
Cry, Cry, Cry... 35
Appalachian Girl... 36
Carlos the Lion 37
A Pirate's Life 38
Mother 40
A Scarecrow Riding the Wind 41
One Voice.. 42
Straw of Pride 43
Cutting Away 44
Dancing with the Mirror.. 45

Finding M 47
And the Tide Rushes In 48
Don't Start the Fire 49
Queen Mother 50
From a Snowman 51
Upon the Midnight Clear 52
At the Morning Light 53
Into the Wide Open Space 54
On a Clear Day 55
Wild Blue 56
Whispering Wind 57
Looking out a Kitchen Window 58
Catskill Way 60
Island in the Bay 61
Snow over Talcott Mountain 62
55 Hurdle Fence 63
Moon over Oak Hill 64
Sunset in Laredo 65
In a Vacant Room 66
Behind the Mask 67
Little Miss Spider 68
A Preacher's Fire 70
Running Away 72
An Everlasting Agreement 73
On the Last Day 75
Steps of Progress 76
In Your Wildest Dreams 77
A Soul 78

Dedicated to my paternal grandmother who out lived all her friends and survived to see the change of life in the air, water and land.

Forward

These poems go into people's everyday emotional conflicts. As you read them they'll take you into the disasters of those lives, the physiological tug of war, the personal indifferences of their actions and the ultimate ending of what they meant.

Our life struggles usually result in striving for personal worth, thriving for self pride and the freedom of being able to make our own decisions. And in the end, do we see ourselves with glee or disdain? Some of us end up in an empty room with the four walls closing in on us and for some, we see life as is and ask why?

For those of us who dream of a better life and ask, why not? We track on as we see ourselves, good or bad. For the rest, they stare at the four walls with no means to survive. With their arms and legs outstretched to stop the walls of life, it's only a matter of time before the walls smother what's left of a thought and ideas.

STRIVING FOR PERSONAL WORTH

Motivation
Confidence
Desire
Adversity
Dare
Risk
Discovery
Solitude
Serenity
Strength
Soar
Reach
Stability

TO CATCH A FALLING STAR

Far beyond the reaches of man
In a galaxy full of illusions
Into the farthest reaches of our mind
Staring into the open space
We stand and wonder

We fathom tranquility
Where we can sleep without concern
Walk without looking
Talk as a voice
Listen without concern

Is it beyond our true expectations
Where we can go out on a clear night
To catch a falling star
To dream the impossible

Is it so far away
Beyond the reaches of mankind
Informing of destiny
But yet, souls are still lost

Is it impossible to dream of hope
To believe in wanting
To have a balance
To reach peace of mind

BORN IN THE FREE WORLD

Life
Unleash upon the world
Go now
Fly free in the frowning face of ignorance
Laugh
Howl as if you've never grow up
Understand this is not a dress rehearsal
This is it
Take it all in
Every single breath
Every last smell
By all means, whatever you do
Use your eyes to see indifference
Use your ears to listen for abuse
Use your mouth to speak words of wisdom
Cry baby cry
A new world awaits you

Principles of Pride

Courtesy
Respect
Participate
Contribute
Excel
Pursue
Innovate
Creativity
Visionary
Sharing
Listen
Communicate

Brings

Self worth
Responsibility
Maturity
Expectations
Happiness

CHIMES OF FREEDOM

Oh say can you see
A flag waives on
15 stars and 15 stripes
Tattered and worn
A birth of a nation

In the beginning, a sight for freedom
Red, white and blue
Independence for a democratic land

The Star Spangled Banner survived bombardment
Pollution
200 years of amendments to a constitution

Forever can you see
By the dawn early light
May you waive forever
To preserve the rights of those who
fought to be free

July 4th represents the day of freedom
Everyday represents the cause of why
we fight the wars of tyranny
To belong
To be US
To be free

Oh say can you see
By the dawn early light
Let the lights blast glare
To let us know the cost of freedom
buried in the sand

WILL SOMEDAY EVER COME

As I walk along life's dirt path
I wonder how I got here
Wondering will someday ever come
To bring a day of wisdom

Not knowing what to do most of the time
I trim the gardens of life branches
In hope of a new flower will bloom

Waiting for the sun to nourish the soil
Enrich the bush to spring up a new blossom
A new beginning of a cycle of beauty

I sit and wait for the new day
Watching and waiting
Hoping someday will come with its new adventures

Let's roll up the sleeves and start digging
Further into god's soil
My hands are dirty with girt
But I'm enlighten by the nourishment of energy

Let's see what the day may bring
Around and around I go
Twirling with the sky
Hoping someday will come

One More Light

Follow me
Across the river
Through the desert
To a sacred land

The leader will preach
Disciples were everywhere
The cabinet was the apostles

A wood cross
Nails in the flesh
On top of a hill
A cause
Justice

A rock is removed
He raised to teach
Love, honor and respect

In a Holy Land
The disease was leprosy
Starvation was among the poor
Adultery was rapid

From the waters edge
To the stormy mountain
The word is spread

One more light to guide us through our trials
One more light to learn the injustices
One more light to forgiveness

TURN THE LIGHT ON

Today
All you sinners
Bare your souls
Cry on your knees

Today and now
All you children running from scruples
Stop and listen to the sound of wisdom
Twist your body around and watch

Today and tomorrow
All you parent's who do not see
Open your eyes and visualize a need
Stop pointing and start paying attention

Now
All who will hear
Turn the light on
Time to listen
Time to talk with the survivors
Pushing them away from the devastation of their life

Today
All us together
Time to place us with those of turbulence
Let's dig a hole and bury our past transgressions
To time capsule a life no more

EMBRACING FOR LIFE

Can the heart beat any harder?
With the heat of the night simmering
Sweat beading down the brow
Twists and turns of bodies swirling like a twister

PASSION

Arms extended
Legs curled
A dead mans grip
Heart and soul delivered instantly
Together as one

CHEMISTRY

Not letting the vision go
Passionate times exist
Knowing one thoughts
Best friends
Embracing for life

A World of Color

One by one
They sing their song
Of honor and shame
Of course and consequences

Young colors of the world
Knowing they're the ones who'll need to
show us the way
Coming together as one
Praising the civilize being

From the top of a mountain
To the ocean floor
From the country ranch
To the city steel

As daylight breaks
Hand link fence has begun
With one voice of concern
A reverberation of communication

It's a time to heal
A time to forgive
A time to repent
A time to care

INTRUDER

Knock knock
I'm here
Wanted or not

Unknown to you
Walking around
Lurking
Soliciting

Don't scream is the thought
Weapon of choice is in the hand
Be still, no one gets hurt

Were should I go?
What should I do?
Be quiet?
Scream?

Eyes watching and waiting
Step by step
Demands made
Turn off the lights

No end in sight
Will this be my last day?
Will this be my last day?

Time is now standing still
Agony exist
Anxiety prevails

Thoughts of love ones come into the mind
My last words
I'm watching and waiting for the moment

Get me out of here
Lost in a nightmare
Watching and waiting

INSIDE THE WALL

Rapists
Murderers
Burglars

All together
Mast in a grey community
Some tougher then others
No one smarter than any other

All surrounded by wire 30 feet high
Curled in a ball
Circling a concrete wall

Men perched atop
Armed and ready to control
Attire all the same
Blue and white, hat in place
This, to tell the difference of protector versus evil

Convicts can't breakdown the wall
A cement courtyard becomes their home
Their fellow jail mates become their friends
Family
Lovers

Destiny has brought them here
Unknown time wasted
They couldn't get out of their own way

Together at last
Soul mates to commiserate
Inside the wall
The only con, is now time

Time spent
Time taken
Time wasted away

CHAIRS

How does one sit in them?
Does one sit to be close to a prospector?
Does one sit in judgement?
Vigilance?
Serenity?
Longing?
Does one sit in protest?
Of terrorism?
Anarchy?
Does one sit with friends?
To talk?
To laugh?
Does the chair ever do the sitting?
Is there any power in sitting?
Do they ever move?
Do they suggest anyone can sit in them?
Do they represent the normal?
The unthinkable?
The explicit?
Will the chair wait?

LOOKING FOR A PEACE OF MIND

Finding a balance through a brain thought is within us all
It can tell you about a hopeless memory
But can't tell you what action to take to resolve
It makes you move towards a vision
But can't tell you how to get there
It informs you to move your feet
But doesn't tell you what path to take
It lets you see where you're stepping
But doesn't tell you how large of a step it is
It tells you to move your limbs for protection
But doesn't tell you from whom you need to protect against

In the black hole of the cell
There's an endless spiral of illusions
A symmetry of thoughts and words
Picking and choosing which means the most to you
is your choice
A selection which will allow you to move comfortably
without disturbing natures balance

A wandering vision
Looking into a void of the misunderstanding
Looking for a concept
Hoping for a moment of contentment

EMPTINESS OF BIRTH

Childless by nature
One born without being
One lasted two years before succumbing

I now look into a void
Day after day
Wondering
Why me?

Maternal nature nagging at my sense of motherhood
Looking at children playing with parents not aware
Walking by with a smile of what could've been

My body is now empty of birth
No more chances for a life given and taken away without cause
I live with the memory of a moment of joy
Now, I live with the thoughts of my purpose
of emptiness of birth

Rejoice people rejoice
For it is you who have life's creation
I, continue to walk and hope my body will not fail me again
One day at a time looking for the purpose
Of emptiness of birth

TERMINALLY ILL

Denial
Anger
Depression
Acceptance
Redemption
Ascension

CRYING FROM HEAVEN

Will you know my name when I'm gone to heaven?
Years of work dissolved in a moment
No more time to create or care

Trying to hang on
No doubt it's over
Will you know my name?

Did you want to see me for the last time?
Did my steps of life mean anything?
Did my words penetrate the embodiment of the circle of life?

I'm crying from heaven
Looking down on the poor souls left behind
No shoulder to lean on
No more hands to reach out

Did you know my name?
Will it forever be kept on your mind?
Water falling from the heavens cleansing the earth
Washing away the footsteps once taken

Out among the stars
The darkness fills the void
Another light for the ages
Another life for the ages to determine why
Footsteps in the sand will slowly wash away
Will you remember my name?

Sierra Leone Amputee

Peace, peace
I hear the city of our nation
After a war which has left behind many atrocities
Come, oh peace, come

I am lonely
No mother
No father
My brothers and sisters have gone astray

My hand has been amputated
Where am I?
Who to live with?
My answer is peace
Come, oh peace, come

A QUAKE IN THE CITY

The city was in ruins
The population was in a panic
Bodies stacking up
Looters being shot
The day was April 18,1906

The financial district was destroyed
Fires were burning all over the city
The wind was shifting
The fires were advancing
Marshall law had been declared

Thousands of panicking citizens
Quickly salvaging household goods they could
They were spending sleepless nights in parks
Open spaces were at a premium

A wondrous city
Shaking and cracking
Crumbling in a moment

A Civilization Savaged

Mothers brush flies from sick children
Lying two and three
On a mattress with rusting iron springs

The halls reek of gasoline which orderlies use to clean floors
It's a cheap solvent in this oil rich nation
Food and medicine have all but disappeared

Families squatting in a cave like room
It's part of a sprawling complex of unfinished buildings
Without sanitation
Running water

This is not living
They have died
Crying in their bowls of rice
A country no longer sending food rations

A decade of deprivation
A people has been devastated
Proud of their rich cultural heritage
Now, they watch their babies died of curable diseases

Families selling heirlooms for food
Artists paint over old canvases
Sculptors search junkyards for bronze
Violinists play on rusted strings

Sanctions are pulling apart the ties, which bind life
Hunger
Disease
Jobs

Mental Illness is on the rise
Child abuse is increasing due to stress
Divorce is the only way out for men
Street crime is uncontrolled

It looks like Nazi Germany
Where the party destroyed the economy
Which in turn lead to fascism

It's not
It's the 21st century in an Arab country
Far from understanding a democratic society
Stalinism at its best

Government letting their civilized world disintegrate
Into the sands of the desert oil
Where the leader has his own causes
Afraid to step outside of his own cave
To face the issues of his people etch on their faces

Echo's of Starvation

My ears still echo
The whimpers of starving children
Anguished mothers crying
Cradling dying sons and daughters

When I close my eyes
I'm haunted by the images of the emaciated
They stare blankly
A silent cry
Feed me
Feed me

Their huge haunting eyes
Look up for compassion
Plead for their empty mouths to be filled

Dying children stagger around in a living nightmare
Dehydrated
Malnourished
Clothes worn and tattered
Desperately seeking shelter
The relentless burning rays of the sun ripping through them

With eyes sunken deep in their sockets
Protruding ribs
Swollen bellies
Such visible misery

The Children grow weaker by the hour
They surely will die a horrible, painful death
Nowhere to be brought
They're left were they lie
A dry river bed
Among the dirt
For the crows to have

IN THE GLOOMING OF THE MOON LIGHT

I walk with my shadow following behind
I notice no one
Walking straight in and around obstacles
My shadow knows what to expect
But no one else does
For where I go and stay is my sanctuary

Walking endlessly to a vacant lot
Turning into a door long gone from its hinges
Water dripping from the rusted pipes
Dodging the wood planks and steel beams long discarded

I sit on a pale upside down looking out among the city buildings
The windows are brown from ages of dirt
Only spots where rain has sprinkled upon them

I pull out my warm needle
It helps me understand life's dilemmas
Sending me into a spiral of happier days

My heart feels the warmth of the hole
I, who sit alone
In a building unfit for man
In a life which has become worthless
In a world not meant for me
Happiness becomes my warm shooter

WALKING INTO AGE

Why am I so down?
It came to me one morning
No interesting new music
Teenagers look younger and younger
No wife
No children
No summer home

I have my books
My music collection of a time gone by
It seems I'm on the other side of life
A place which eventually shows up for everyone

How important is it to reconstruct a life
Being involved is utmost
Having a say
Keeping the world around me moving forwards

It seems I'm losing the grip to the next generation
I see nothing more than young adults not knowing enough
Did our parents see the same?

I've become older than the world around me
Could it be maturity has crept into my life?
Peter Pan no more
Playtime has ended
It's time to construct a suitable ending
A new gift on life

Wisdom
Knowledge
Sharing the light
The rocking chair in the corner waits

CRY, CRY, CRY

Water rolling down the cheeks
An emotional release
No words spoken

It's a release unexpected
Listening to someone
Watching something
A sixth sense prevails

An inner thought
A response to self realization
A response to knowing, but never spoken

An unknown to men and women
Tear ducts open
An expression released
Crying

APPALACHIAN GIRL

Flowers in her hair
Walking down her muddy driveway
Mountain terrain around her filled the sky with gray granite

A home with holes in the roof
Water from the universal well
An outhouse was in the distance

Brown hair girl dancing with the wind
Eyes of blue
Cheekbones chiseled from the greek gods

Spirit always cheerful
Learning everyday to hope
Keeping an eye on change
Thinking of the future

Cold winters
Wood stove for warmth
Dreary Spring and Fall's
Pails laid down to catch the falling rain

Breezy summers
Time to run barefoot across the yellow field of grain
Swings of emotion
Never worrying about her surroundings
Everyday is one day closer to the day
of leaving her penitentiary

CARLOS THE LION

Music from the heart
Unity is his cry
His guitar gently weeps
Samba Pa Ti

What is your name was the question
Gathering around to sing of praise
Listening to the latin riffs

A small lion in height
Tall in voice
Words playing under the Havana moon
A caravan brings him and his mates across the land
A simple word to a dysfunctional family

Supernatural was smooth
A black magic women strolls on through
A sacrifice of the soul

Play on little lion
Rip through us all
Lioness people are lining up to hear
a soul sacrificed

Play on little lion
Signify unity
Harmony
Peace

Walk on Carlos
One riff after another
A verse for all to comprehend
A sound to breathe into our inner being

A Pirate's Life

A pirate looks into the distance
His followers are parrot heads
His place of drink is Margaritaville

Sailing along with banana boats
A guitar in his hand
Singing on beaches
Bars
Boats

What a life he has
From white sand beaches
To a stool in a bar
Walking around in shorts
Colorful shirts

Singing about what he sees
From a bar he called his own
To Christmas in the Caribbean
To cheeseburgers in paradise

He had a vision
Of what he wanted in life
Never giving in to normalcy
He pucks his guitar to all sights of life

His concerts are feeding frenzies
Older adults wearing strange head gear
Wishing they could live a beach life

What a wonderful world to be in
Come along and sing songs
Among rum sizzlers
Vats of margarita's
Reaching into a world of masquerades

A pirate's love and luck
In one particular harbor
Come Monday
No where to go
Just trying to reason with a hurricane season

MOTHER

Mother what did you hear?
Mother what can we say
Mother can you say you care

Mother can you hear them crying
Mother can you see them begging
Mother why do we kill

Mother why do you have vices?
Mother why do you believe you're not worthwhile?
Mother try to understand

Mother try to stand straight
Mother try to be forthright
Mother try to comfort us

Mother why do tears come to our eyes?
Mother why does our skin burn?
Mother why did we drop the bomb?

Mother tell us why we were born
Mother lead us away from damnation
Mother lead us away from pandora
Mother tell us you'll spread your arms
and keep us all

Mother

A Scarecrow Riding the Wind

Once upon a time
I used to know this scarecrow
Cast alone between the furrows
In a field no longer sown by anyone
I held a dandelion
That said, the time had come
To leave upon the wind
Let the birds re-seed the field
So a new beginning can be grown

ONE VOICE

Slowly moving closer
Lurking in the shadows of doubt
A climatic moment
Not ready to reveal its essence

A disagreement brings it further along
Debating your views, watching it closely
A stance keeps it moving in like a train
Stubbornness brings it to the forefront

A difference of opinion brings its to a swirl
Forgiveness is not mentioned until the end
Only the partners will know to finish

Best friends and lovers are often mixed as one
Ever so often they need to be separated
A clear mind is needed to discover
One voice
So it can be heard

STRAW OF PRIDE

They've been praying for you every night
They want desperately to tell a story
They can't tell you themselves

Imagine
To believe you're completely someone different
Someone you'd never wanted to be

It's dawn and you're sixteen years old
Your mother gently shakes you
You had a restless sleep

Your sibling remains asleep beside you
Weakened from a severe case of an incurable disease
Your mother's attention must lie with the sibling

In your subconscious you know your mother is tired
Her hope fading
Would she turn elsewhere if the sibling were not ill

You move from your bed of straw
Wander out of the one room shelter
You join other children in the field
You'll labor in the heat until sundown

Only a piece of bread while you work
You concentrate on the work at hand
The wage is only good enough for corn bread
Enough for your sibling to last another day

You learn not to cry
You swallow your pride
You pray for your brother
And for the night, the nightmares to disappear

Cutting Away

What did we know
Nothing more than what's in our mind
From passion to chemistry

What did we know
A past long gone
Right woman, wrong time
Wrong place, right woman

What did we know
Words can not express our vision
Living worlds apart
Hearts beating within

What did we know
Walking and waiting for the sun to set
Children never became us

How did we get here
Passion
Desire
Hope
Wanting

And in the end
Stepping away with a sigh
Driving down a lonely road
Cutting away from the obvious
Looking into a world of absence

DANCING WITH THE MIRROR

I'm bored with myself
My attitude needs a change
My clothes are old and worn
I'm tired of being alone

I just want a little magic
A little comfort to spring me into action
A bounce in my step
A glancing look by someone

I'm tired of looking at myself
Just dancing to the mirror
Alone in my thoughts
Waiting for a reflection

Shaking back and forth
Waiting for no one in particular
Just dancing to the mirror
Around and around

Mirror, mirror
I'm a little worried
A bit taken back by what I see
I need some inspiration

Dancing to the mirror
A hand comes out to reach me
A radiant glow
A twirl around
Just me & my reflection

I finally see myself
A new world abound
Joyous sounds are not that of what I am
But, of who I am

Dancing to the mirror
I see a reflection of courage and ambition
I see my eyes are clear and straight
I'm twirling around and around into a being of persistency

FINDING M

Not long ago in a far distance past
There was a woman who stood by her emotional needs
Stringing herself out piece by piece to those whom would want her
She twirled and twirled as persons pulled on these strings

Around and around her head a dizzying array of words
Not knowing any better she stopped only to determine
her time and destination
Not finding a way to dignify a response to those words spoken
She laughed and danced some more

What was a dysfunctional life
Is now disarray of mental capacity
Right foot, left foot
One in front of the other
Walking through a pasture of gold

Why she thought no one would ever reach her standard of living
is bent to those who knew her
Arms raised up high reaching for the heavens
Looking for answers
Nothing is being returned
A shout could be heard in the distance, Why me?

David C. Putnam

And the Tide Rushes In

Every night
I've been searching you in my dreams
I build you up
You knock me down like I was made of clay

Then the tide rushes in
And washes my dreams away
Then I'm really not sure
Which side of the bed I should lay

You keep looking for someone
To tell your troubles to
I sit down and lend an ear
Yet, I hear nothing new

Crows circling overhead
Observing what's below
Never landing, keeping their wings spread wide

I, watch the acorns fall to the ground
Next, is to stay and watch them grow
As the tide rushes in
And tries to wash my castle away
I sit and ponder
Is it a vision or is it a destiny realized

DON'T START THE FIRE

I'm crying to myself
Sitting and waiting for them to pick me up
Staring and wondering
How did I get this way?
I'm just tired of myself

Looking out the window
My mind stares into the wilderness which doesn't exist
Now I'm just a flame burning endlessly
A fire within boiling my blood

Don't start the fire
The burning has already begun
Keeping the flames burning is a masquerade
I just don't know what to do with myself

Wondering aloud
How did I get this way?
I just need someone to help me out

Twisting and turning myself inside out
I'm just crazy with jealousy
Unless you can dose the flame
Don't start the fire

Queen Mother

Her home is her country
Her children are her countrymen
Her farmhouse is her sanctuary

She has a rage which sprouts at a moments notice
It attacks at the person who goes against her personal beliefs
In ancient time it would be off with your head
Today, its consent wailing

You stand in silence waiting for the end
When it ends you wonder what caused the rage
Long in conviction
Her desire to be queen of her home and life pursuits
outweighs all other intrusions

Men are not wanted
Peace of mind and a piece of land are all she seeks
Away from everyday life
Away from peoples hustle
Away from life's arrogance's
Queen M sits and watches her life walking away into tranquility

FROM A SNOWMAN

Accessories bring me to life
Three snowballs in one body
A top hat from the masters tux assemble
Charcoal from the barbecue pit
Grampa's corn cob pipe stolen from its holder
Buttons from the clothing item not needed anymore
And here I am
The every persons snowman

With a broom in one hand
And a wave of the other
There's nothing stopping me
Just hanging out in the front yard

There I sit
Day after day on cold wintry days
Never sleeping
Standing guard
Waiting for the sun to melt my wide bottom away

I'm happy until the temperature reaches freezing
Once this happens I dissolve into a watery mess
No need to clean me up
I'll just wait until the next wintry day
With snow mounting up once again

Ode to a snowman
A life of always wearing white
A heavy midsection
A wide bottom
But always a jolly happy soul

Upon the Midnight Clear

Once again its time to gather
Upon the midnight clear
To sing and laugh about our time together
To say 'peace on earth good will toward men'
And have some candy canes
Champagne
And those Spanish tropical drinks

They come along by sleigh and reindeer
Horse and carriage
Or any other mode of transportation for the winter roads

We come together after those who gave thanks have eaten the turkey
And the time before going out to the meet the masses for that favorite gift

To listen to those sounds of Christmas
Silver bells chiming, chorus's singing on high
The children asking for everything under the sun
And of course our favorite sound of Grinch and
IT'S MIND pounding into our minds

So before we all get involved with the conceited
The disinterested
The boorish
We come together upon the midnight clear
For a fine Irish Christmas Party
Green tinsel I'm sure
A very fine evergreen tree to adore
With a cold wind howling
And a fire blazing up the chimney so high
Lights twinkling in the distance for delight
And singing 'God Rest Ye Gentleman' to the morning light

AT THE MORNING LIGHT

Sunrise
At the mountain top
On the highest peak
At the first ray light
Just the two of us
Together
With mother nature
God
And the person who'll serve to bring us together

As the first ray of light strikes us both
Stating our vows for eternally
Nature holding still for a moment
Witnessing a bonding forever
The mountainous range embraces us both
On our first day of hope

INTO THE WIDE OPEN SPACE

As far as I can see
Blue skies and summer wind
A horizon in the far off distance
Curving down under
A reflection of three dimension
Trees swaying slightly to the left
Dust particles slowly forming a circular pattern

Twilight sun beams narrowing working their way through
the valleys of the mountain terrain
The rock cliffs billow up into the blue sky
Sharpening their claws for another daring day

ON A CLEAR DAY

The trees are a dull green
The ground is covered in white
The sky is crystal blue
I can see for miles

Beyond the highest peaks of the mountains
Into the valleys so low
The landscape rolling along from hill to hill
Looking like an artist canvas waiting for the next brush of paint

Wondering aloud I can hear my words reaching out
Into the vast countryside echoing beyond my farthest imagination
My arms are outstretch reaching for the day to grasp me
My eyes can visualize a day like no other

Walking into the warmth of the sun
Sunglasses relaxing the eyes
An easy peaceful feeling
On a clear day

WILD BLUE

A day clear with a baby blue sky
A gentle breeze covers us
with clear fresh air
White fluffy clouds slowly wander by
Birds soaring high

Sounds of morning has broken cracked
the sunrise
The mountains stretching up trying to
reach the sky limits
Unlimited in its serene effect
Nothing will interfere with its day's work
Leaving us with a moment of reflection

Come with me wild blue
Let me gather your energy to live another day
Your strength to visually see mother natures beauty
Your warmth to understand life's misgivings

WHISPERING WIND

Gently brushing through the leaves
A whistle to let us know its here
Circling about
Swirling
Moving from here to there

A cool evening breeze
A window opens
The wind sweeps through
Leaving a cool sensation
Revitalized

The sky is baby blue
Clouds meander about
Floating by with no concern
A perfect evening
With a whispering wind trailing about

Looking out a Kitchen Window

A farmhouse
On top of a hill
A small kitchen window
A view to a vast open space

Five acres to review
Green grass to mow
A gray barn for storage

My eyes peer to the left
A mountain stands in the distance
Tall and majestic
Reaching up into the sunrays of the day

Trees a of different sort surround the grounds
Old bark which has turned to gray
They've stood the test of time

A garden undone
Dead weeds and brown moss have come together
Waiting for a rake to teeth its unearthing

A wooden pole stands a mist in the field
of yellow grain
A crows perch for sure
Waiting for the prey to approach

A gentle wind covers it all
Brushing the loose grass over the field
The trees sway in unison as if dancing to a waltz

As I walk away from the kitchen window
I know mother earth will continue to sculpture
the landscape without me
Creating, changing and enduring
Everyday
Without human intervention

Catskill Way

Out along the hillside
Among the valley of green trees
Farmers ploy away a season

Hay will be stacked
Soil will be turned
A harvest will be completed

You can look out to majestic peaks
surrounding you
To view a land which time has forgotten
Where the wind swirls between the hills
And the stream waters cool to ice blue

As a way of life, slow and methodical
A wave of a hand by an unknown person as you pass by
A language all their own
No distrust among them
Only neighbors helping each other

My land is your land has meaning here
They live in God's country
To graze and nurture for each growing season

Chickens and hens
Deer's and fawns
Foxes and wolves
All walk among the hay of gold

All will peer up to see a wanderer or two
A red fox will trot by with no glance of concern
Wolves will howl at night to no particular sight

In the valley
For which time has forgotten
The men and women of this lost land
Push along with no watch to keep it's pace
Just a day and a night
To finish a chore which starts on each morning light

ISLAND IN THE BAY

Among the swirling winds rippling across
the gray ocean water
A mist in the bay
On a cold summer day
With white & gray clouds hovering above
Standing alone
Brown and desolate
An island made of rock and clay

No way to reach except by a water vehicle
A lighthouse stands guard against intruders
Seagulls look around for upcoming breezes

The gray rocks hold together
Creating a fortress against mother natures
worst conditions

Through rain
Snow
Ice
Wind
The island prevails
Preserving a home for those creatures who fly
with the wind
Or swim among the waves

Snow over
Talcott Mountain

On a cold cloudy day in winter
A storm was brewing from the south valley
Sending the living creatures back into their burrows

Trees so bare they shiver for warmth
The gray clouds hover above massing their energy
Snow already covering a brown dreary landscape

With the snow flakes falling one after another
Attaching themselves to the limbs of trees
The stone wall protecting property lines
The picket fence to the red sled in the backyard

The mountainside disappears into a cloud of white mist
A rolling white sheet covers everything in its path
What was once a brown barren land is now full of
soft white flakes
Piling up to the front door steps
Waiting for someone to sweep it away

The valley waits for the snow to end
People huddling in front of the fireplace
Thinking of how they need to survive

55 HURDLE FENCE

A sprawling acre
A yard of forest green lawn
No garden in sight
Trees here and there to add a New England feel

A three floor colonial
Add a two car garage for all the
necessities of maintenance tools
An attic above for storage

A stone driveway
A lamppost in front to guide your entrance
A tree house built thirty yards in the backyard woods

A kitchen of soldiers
A Fathers' den fit for a king
A reck room for the children to pound away at

The Living Room large enough to hold family gatherings
The Dining Room set up with an oak table and chairs

Sliding doors to the patio
The patio made of slate slabs
Folding chairs were in a circle
Conversations going back and forth

The backyard would be the playground of dreams of heroic play
A Home Run hit to the top of the roof
A goal scored through two trees standing side by side
A touchdown pass thrown between the great oaks
Floodlights lit up the field of dreams for atmosphere

A home
Opened up to all family and friends
No one was denied entry
At 55 Hurdle Fence

MOON OVER OAK HILL

A clear night
A sky falling on top of you
A full moon watches over the valley

As the mountain stretches out along the range
The creatures of the night begin to sound off
A road has been deserted
Only the street line lays flat among the blackness
of the night

Lights filter through a window
Shedding a sparkle of possible life along main street
No human movement
Just a stare and a glance
of an unknown stranger in town

The white post office with its wooden
doors stands on the corner
The church of worship with its steeple so high
is across the street
The old tavern on the green no longer exist
The American flag is folded up for the night

An old town
Traditional in manner
Waiting for no one
Where shadows of history lay in the ground

SUNSET IN LAREDO

The red dust rises above the dry earth
A hundred-degree day turns into a ninety
degree evening
Marlboro men on their saddles stare out into
the canyon of red clay
Dirt covering them from head to toe
Gloves tightly curled around a rope
holding their palomino in place

The sun sits just above the horizon
A bright orange glow bristles through the red dust
The prairie relaxes after a dry sun baking day

The creatures of the land slowly start to move about
Nipping at tumbleweed
Scratching at cactus for liquid

A long day in Laredo
Cowboys herding cattle to their destination
Branding for property rights

Dust on their hats
Lines of age on their faces
Scratchy voices from the dry day
Slowly walking towards the red river valley

Looking out over the valley
The sun setting over the canyon clay
No voices can be heard
As they sit and watch the end of another day
Arms stretched across the neck of their horses
The sun sets beyond the horizon of Laredo,
of the red river valley

IN A VACANT ROOM

Space
No furniture
Dust balls rolling along into the corners
With the wind pushing them up and down
Up
and down

Footprints in the floor
They belong to someone
The same pace
The same walk
Circling
Circling
Circling about

Distant movement
Far away from thinking
A vacant room does not have a breath

The air is cold
The breath from your mouth blows smoke upward
Filtering about among the rafters
Rolling into extinction

You can hear yourself think
Listening to your mind
Your thoughts expand to the size of the room
No pollution noise to stray you away

Standing in emptiness
Staring out into the sunlight streaming in
Waiting for the lonely room to speak

What was?
What is?
What will become?

BEHIND THE MASK

Let it be known the mask covers flaws
For it raises the mystery of who you are
You can walk along with no one taking notice
Persona raises to another distinction

For it be told
A short time in duration
If the illusion continues
You're masquerading
There's no truth

For it be told
You're withholding untold ills
A deceiving character
It's not your own
Gravely walking about
Looking like a nomad

Who are you?
The truth will be known
When the mask is disposed

LITTLE MISS SPIDER

Born to web
A soul larger than life
No one expected a panther approach to life

Walking continuously
She surrounded her family foundation
Her disposition dissolved into functionality of a web

A mind of her own
Straight forward with glee
She moved with hie
Holes developed everywhere

Day after day
A climb out of each hole
No hole was large enough to contain her
No road long enough to walk
Little Miss Spider walked along with determination

Solitude is what brought calm
Slow down, don't move so fast
She held onto her virtues
Even though those around her did not

Condemn the demons
Pray to the lord
Save me what you will
Give me strength to chose righteously

A life in peril
Never ending story
She has the ideas
There will be a time for resurrection

To begin again
Cleansing the mind
To see for miles ahead
No clouds to impede her way

Marching on
Only strength is waiting
Nothing will cross her path
Only her thoughts will intervene
a serene vista

A Preacher's Fire

He pursued relentlessly
Calling and knocking at her door
Night after night

Why not was his call
Why was hers
Back and forth with debating a sin
A devil appeared night after night

The soul of her slowly started to give in
He pursued more aggressively
She prayed for help
Night after night

Sin in waiting
Demons surrounding the home
Angels had no control
The devil wanted her more than ever
Night after night

She finally gave in
Hoping the devil would go away
He preyed on her insecurity
Night after night

He of marriage and children
Her a single parent
He's the lord leader of poor shepherds
She part of the flock
He's oversees commitment and strengthening of those most in need
She dreams of hope

She cries at night wondering how she became the way she is
He comforts her and whispers words of encouragement
Hollow as they are she holds on believing

They came together for no other reason than hope
She can't control her insecurities
Loneliness
Her desire to be loved

He loses his way from the flock
Condescending
Deceiving as he goes

For one night of sin
He loses his flock
She becomes a sorceress
With a demon for a baby

The lord takes it away
For it is not hers to keep
For it belongs to him for nourishing

For him, a Pastor of dishonor
His wife leaves him in search of a new true light
His flock leaves him where the fire burns

For one night of sin
A world of two lives turned into hell
Wandering souls looking for hope and belief

Running Away

A sigh
A gasp
A whimper

Thinking about what has been said
Not knowing why they've said it
Thinking, this isn't what should be done
Listening, but not

Why me?
I don't belong here
I'm not like them
Turning away and demonstrating temperament

A thought comes over me
Come on family, what could you be thinking
Running up the stairs
Closing the bedroom door
Flinging myself onto the bed
Looking up in belittlement
I'm just a child
How could I know what they're talking about?

To many words
Not enough answers
A smile overcomes my face
A blank stare into the ceiling

Running away from my thoughts
Running away from my
Running away from
Running away
Running
R

An Everlasting Agreement

The summer ended
They said their good byes
He drove by the majestic landscape
Making his trips to her enjoyable

It started with two individuals
Similar demeanors
Respecting one another
Loving each other
Trying to find a way to stay together

Wishing to have an understanding mind
Wishing to understand the dynamics of
each social situation
Wishing not to express emotions verbally

At last, they walked away
Stoic and understanding
Harmless and peaceful outside
Kicking and crying inside

Never regretting the reunion decision
Better to have tried
Than not tried at all and wonder forever

Routine and logic follows the man
Last minute decisions and micro managing the woman
Chemistry and passion followed them both
No resolution ever came about

Too careful?
To independent?
To busy to get in touch with their true emotions?
Time will only know

This is a love story
Had
Lost
Had again
Lost again

A summer of romance
Passion
Adventure
Turning into an autumn lifestyle once was
and is again
Out of sync and transient
Yet, they call their own

They'll keep in touch
Support one another
Through their good, bad and indifferent decisions

And in the end they can only hope for destiny
For a new beginning
A new heart
An everlasting agreement to be one

ON THE LAST DAY

Tomorrow will come
I sit and wait for the call
Day after day
Hoping it'll never come

At times we were intimate
Choosing words carefully
The years of wisdom had no place in our existence
Knowing an outstretch hand was always there
Not saying the words we wanted to hear
Afraid it might scare us away

Tomorrow
We knew it wouldn't last forever
It had to end someday
I just wanted to be here to say good bye

Tomorrow
I will be there with a hand
Sincere and breathless
Whispering 'don't leave me'
Words can not express the emptiness

Tomorrow
On your last day
I just want to say good bye
I just want to say good bye

Steps of Progress

Catch a falling star
Never let it go
For its up to you to motivate yourself
Climb the steps of progress
You can never understand the principles
You can understand the method
Stepping forwards
Lean in
Touch life's gifts
It's all within your means

IN YOUR WILDEST DREAMS

Beyond your wildest dreams
There stands a place of yore
Between what we believe in
And what we know

It's colorful in design
Washed cleaned every night
Sun splash-yellow rays rain down on you
Red brick walkways extend as far as you can see

Unfortunately we come to see another world
Cruel and unjust
When the people of excess turn us around
Twirling into dizziness
We lay down and let them walk

In your wildest dreams did you think success would be easy?
Did you think raising a family would be like yesterday?
Did you think life would be so engaging?

Come into the world of living nightmares
Where we think what should be, but isn't
Where we see things which are, but should never be

A Soul

In a life
There's only one person you can rely on
Yourself
Self worth goes to the soul in us all
Direction
Perseverance
Character